Walks on
Canna, Rùm, Eigg and Muck

Walks on
Canna, Rùm, Eigg and Muck

by

Mary Welsh

Maps and Illustrations by
Christine Isherwood

Westmorland Gazette, Kendal, Cumbria

First published 1996

ISBN 0 902272 97 7

© Westmorland Gazette, 1996

Published by
Westmorland Gazette
22 Stricklandgate, Kendal, Cumbria

Printed by
Miller Turner Printers Limited
The Sidings, Beezon Fields, Kendal, Cumbria

Foreword

This book is about the Small Isles - Canna, Rùm, Eigg and Muck - four islands forming a single parish. They are linked by Caledonian MacBrayne's steamer *Lochmor* and share one doctor, resident on Eigg.

Yet each island is different. Rùm is particularly so for, while the other three are formed of basalt rock, Rùm has no basalt and so the topography and vegetation are unique. Rùm is a nature reserve, while Canna, Eigg and Muck are more fertile and are agricultural. The members of Rùm's community, associated with the reserve, come for a time and leave. On the other three islands, some at least of the inhabitants have lived there all their lives.

The islands differ in membership too. Canna is owned by the National Trust for Scotland, Rùm by Scottish Natural Heritage and Eigg by a German artist. Only on Muck do the owners, the MacEwens, live and work on the island, representing 99 years of continuous ownership.

This is a book for the visitor, who has an important part to play in the economy of these islands. With our wide horizons and ever-changing weather, many of the walks described here can be truly spectacular. Even I, who have lived here for 54 years, never cease to be amazed by the beauty of the scene.

I am sure you will be too.

Good walking.

Lawrence MacEwen

Acknowledgments

I received much help in producing this book and my grateful thanks go to my friend Maureen Fleming for her help in researching and checking the walks; to Christine Isherwood, who has illustrated them so delightfully, encouraging walkers to seek out the sights for themselves; to William Kindness of Caledonian MacBrayne and Murdo Grant of Arisaig Marine Limited for their kindly support; to the Fort William Tourist Board, who gave me friendly help and advice, to Jean Cowling for her careful copy-editing, and to my husband Tom for his constant support. My thanks also go to the following, who kindly looked at parts of the manuscript and gave me invaluable help: Mrs J L Campbell of Canna; Ian MacIntyre of the National Trust for Scotland; Dr Alison MacLennan of the RSPB; Martin Curry, Manager of the Rùm Reserve. Finally, wholehearted thanks go to Lawrence MacEwen who looked at the whole manuscript and wrote the preface.

Author's Note

Please remember on all these walks:

Wear suitable clothes and take adequate waterproofs.

Walk in strong footwear; walking boots are advisable.

Carry the relevant map and know how to use it.

Take extra food and drink as emergency rations.

Carry a whistle; remember six long blasts repeated at one minute intervals is the distress signal.

Do not walk alone, and tell someone where you are going.

If mist descends, return.

Close all gates. Respect walls and fences.

Where dogs are allowed, keep them under close control.

Readers are advised that while the author has taken every effort to ensure the accuracy of this guidebook, changes can occur after publication. You should check locally on transport, accommodation, etc. The publisher would welcome notes of any changes. Neither the publisher nor the author can accept responsibility for errors, omissions or any loss or injury.

Location Map

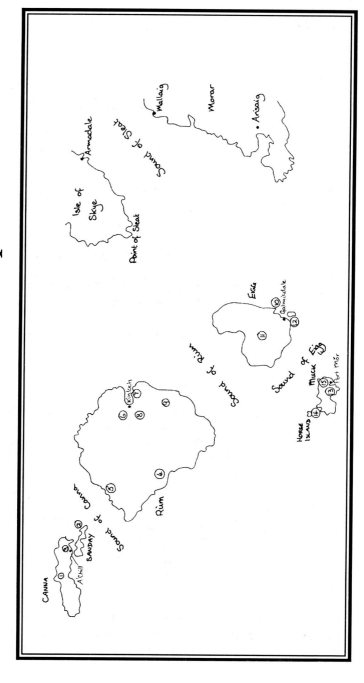

Canna

Canna is a green island with rocky outcrops and with high and low cliffs. In 1981, it was given to the National Trust for Scotland by Dr and Mrs J L Campbell of Canna House.

The island lies north-west of Rùm, Eigg and Muck and to the south-west of Skye. The Caledonian MacBrayne ferry calls at Canna on its way to the other small isles. It visits several days of the week and sometimes stays for an hour at the deep-water pier.

Canna has no metalled road but provides much pleasing walking.

For information on the sailings, telephone Caledonian MacBrayne on 01687 462403.

Rùm

Rùm has a dozen fine mountains and much rough moorland, and reveals itself to those approaching by sea as extremely rugged. There are no metalled roads. Two stony tracks lead from Kinloch village, one to Harris and the other to Kilmory. There are several pony tracks.

Rùm is owned by Scottish Natural Heritage and is a National Nature Reserve. The reserve welcomes everyone but the island is not developed for tourism. It is primarily managed to maintain its outstanding natural heritage value and to encourage greater awareness of that value through education and quiet enjoyment - including walking.

Walkers can obtain hostel or hotel accommodation at Kinloch Castle, self-cater in a number of basic village properties and also use two remote bothies. There is a

7

campsite in Kinloch, but for management and safety reasons there is no camping in the wild. Visitors must arrange their accommodation before they arrive. They are requested to file route cards at the Reserve Office if they are walking on the island, though this does not imply responsibility on the part of Scottish Natural Heritage - merely to assist them should voluntary search parties be required.

Caledonian MacBrayne ferries from Mallaig visit Loch Scresort and then visitors transfer to a motor launch to reach the pier. Murdo Grant of Arisaig Marine, Arisaig, runs an efficient and refreshing service to the island, though this is seasonal and confirmation of sailing is advisable.

For information on days and times of sailings, telephone Caledonian MacBrayne on 01687 462403, and Arisaig Marine on 01687 450678.

Arisaig Marine trips enable visitors from Arisaig to tour the castle, though days and times do vary. For information about the castle, check direct on 01687 462037.

Further information and accommodation details may be obtained from the Reserve Office, The White House, Rùm; telephone 01687 462026.

Eigg

From the mainland, An Sgurr, Eigg's great pitchstone lava block, is seen dominating the island, towering over green pastures, heather moorland and the high platform of Beinn Bhuidhe. From neighbouring Rùm and Muck, Eigg seems just a step over the sea.

The island has one road that runs north-south and divides in two at each end. Visit the glorious curving Bay of Laig and the famous singing sands at Sgiotaig Bay. Look for an ancient cross at Kildonnan and dramatic sea caves on the south shore.

Several times a week Caledonian MacBrayne's passenger ferry lies off Castle Island and a motor launch transports visitors to the pier. Murdo Grant's boat, *Shearwater*, from Arisaig Marine, calls at the pier regularly throughout the summer.

For information, telephone Caledonian MacBrayne on 01687 462403, and Arisaig Marine on 01687 450678.

Muck

Muck is a small, delightfully peaceful, friendly island, which lies three miles off Eigg and measures two miles by one. It has hay meadows, cattle pastures, moorland and a steepish hill, Beinn Airein (451 feet).

The Caledonian MacBrayne passenger ferry and Arisaig Marine both run services to Port Mór. Skerries shelter the harbour, but present a hazard for boats entering in rough weather.

The island is mainly owned by Lawrence MacEwen, who is also the farmer. He allows camping on request. His brother, Ewen, part-owner of the island, runs a reasonably priced hotel, and will also recommend bed and breakfast accommodation. There is a good craft shop and fine tea room.

The island has one road, which runs from the pier to the farm at Gallanach, situated on the north-west coast of the island. Close by is Horse Island, reached on foot at low tide.

For information telephone Lawrence MacEwen, farmer, on 01687 462362 and Ewen MacEwen, hotelier on 01687 462365.

Contents

Walk Number		Miles	Page Number
1	Circular Walk around the Coast of Canna	5 ¹/₂	11
2	Circular Walk around Sanday	5 ¹/₂	15
3	Circular Walk to a Celtic Cross and Standing Stone, Canna	2	18
4	Linear Walk to Harris on Rùm	13	21
5	Circular Walk towards Guirdil, Rùm	12	24
6	Circular Walk through Kinloch Glen, Rùm	2 ¹/₂	27
7	Linear Walk along South Side, Loch Scresort, Rùm	3 ¹/₂	30
8	Linear Walk to Coire Dubh, Rùm	3	33
9	Linear Walk to Dibidil, Rùm	11 - 15	35
10	Linear Walk to Kildonnan, Eigg	3	39
11	Circular Walk to An Sgurr and Cleadale, Eigg	11	42
12	Circular Walk to Caves, Eigg	2	47
13	Circular Walk to Beinn Airein, Muck	4 ¹/₂ - 5	50
14	Linear Walk to Horse Island, Muck	3 ¹/₂	53
15	Circular Walk round the Eastern End of Muck	2 ¹/₂	56

1. A Circular Walk around the Coast of Canna

Information

Distance:	5 ½ miles
Time:	3 hours
Map:	Pathfinder Canna NG20, Landranger 39 Rùm and Eigg
Terrain:	This is a challenging and sometimes rough walk. Choose a good day when there is little wind. Walking boots essential. The National Trust for Scotland asks that you do not climb to the little building on An Coroghon; the very steep way is badly eroded and dangerous. Do not descend or climb any of Canna's cliffs, the rock is very soft. Many apparent paths are made by sheep and goats.

No dogs are allowed on the island.

This glorious walk takes you over the high platform of tertiary basalt of Canna, where the open rolling pastures are deserted except for Cheviot sheep and some cattle. Canna itself lies two to three miles north-west of Rùm, and for much of this walk you feel that island's forbidding presence.

Walk the track from the pier, passing the Presbyterian church with its round tower and ornate gate. Turn right. Overhead you might see Canna's golden eagle. Stride the well-reinforced walled track, where basalt columns tower high above the delightful woodland of Canna House. Pass through the gate on the left, opposite the barn. Walk right,

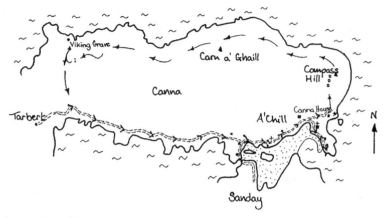

along the edge of the pasture.

Follow the fence as it edges a small wood. Pass through the next gate and walk onto a rocky shore to view a stack named Prison Rock, An Coroghon, which lies to your right. Look high up to see a tiny stone hut, called a castle on the Ordnance Survey map, which is approached by a very steep track. Here, in about 1666, a chief of the Clanranald imprisoned his wife to prevent her seeing her lover, a MacLeod of Skye.

Return to the last gate and pass through. Turn right and climb beside the fence, on your right. Go through the next gate and continue beside the ravine on your left. Where the trees cease, turn right and, after 100 yards, bear right to view groups of stones, all that remain of several shielings. Beyond, climb straight up onto Compass Hill, so named because the iron in the rock

Prison Rock

distorted the compasses of ships. Place your compass on several outcrops and find out for yourself. Look down with care for a spectacular view of the harbour, Sanday, the old Roman Catholic Church and the houses along the shore.

Press on northwards and then north-west along the flower-covered pasture, keeping well away from the sheer cliff edges. Follow the sheep trods that take you the easiest way. Use the stile to climb the fence, pausing here to look across the sea to the Cuillin of Skye.

Take the good paths through the heather, avoiding the wet areas flagged with cottongrass. keep beside the fence as it protects you and the sheep from an immensely steep ravine. Walk the narrow path along the upper reaches of the gorge to a point where it is easy and safe to cross.

Climb straight up closely hugging the rocks on your left to avoid more steep-sided ravines. Then the way begins to descend. Pause to look back at the sheer basalt cliffs over which you have just walked. Further on, down to your left, there is a wall. Descend and follow it, first right (west) and then as it curves left (south) inland. Look for a south-facing slope, the home of many rabbits, close to the wall. Here you can see two souterrains. These are Bronze-Age subterranean earth houses, perhaps used for storage or shelter. The entrance in both has a stone lintel. You can just wriggle inside.

Greylag Geese

Cross the wall to continue (west) and pass, on a green sward, the stone remnants of an Iron-Age settlement. Then swing right towards the cliff edge. Do not descend the sheer ravine dropping down to the sea, but go on right (east). Follow a clear path that leads to the edge of a shallow cliff, overlooking a large apron of low-lying land. Stand on the cliff for a good view below of an arrangement of boulders that is long and narrow and faces north west. This is known as a Viking grave and because of its shape may have contained a boat. It is also known locally as the grave of the King of Norway.

Retrace your steps to return to the two Bronze-Age subterranean earth houses. Go on downhill to a track that starts near a ruined croft, Tarbert, beside which is a large barn. Walk left along this gated track. After nearly two miles, with grand views all the way, take the left branch where the tracks divide to return to the pier. If you walk this track in the late evening, you stand a chance of seeing Manx Shearwaters on the wing.

2. A Circular Walk around Sanday

Information

Distance:	5 ½ miles from the pier
Time:	3 hours
Map:	Pathfinder Canna NG20, Landranger 39 Rùm and Eigg
Terrain:	Easy walking but can be wet. Boots advisable.

A lovely walk to which you will wish to return.

Sanday projects east from Canna like a long arm and gives good shelter to the natural deep harbour and pier. Between Canna and Sanday the water drains out on the ebb, leaving just a trickle at the west end. The track from the pier, suitable for vehicles, ends at a footbridge, frequently washed away but first built by the parish council in 1905. It links the two islands. Beyond the bridge an unreinforced track continues and at low tide vehicles cross the channel to gain access to it, to reach the houses and school on Sanday.

Walk the track beyond the footbridge. On the shore, hoodie crows pick up crustaceans and drop them from a height, then down they swoop to eat the exposed soft parts.

Continue past several empty houses and the small school - one room in the teacher's house. Go on, and when you come to a pasture, where lie rusting implements used decades ago, take a gently rising path away from the shore. Head on

15

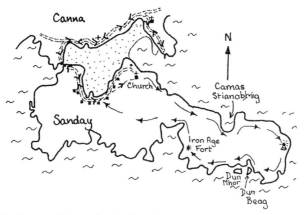

towards the striking Catholic church ahead. It stands
aloof and distinctive in a walled enclosure and has
been replaced for services by a small building
on the other side of the channel. Go inside the
listed building, constructed in 1885, and look
for the Thompson mouse on the communion
rail. The church has a round-headed entrance
and a rectangular three-storey tower, and its
prominence made it a useful guide to
returning fishermen.

Leave the church by a gate
in the wall and continue in
a clockwise direction
above the shoreline.
Just offshore, grey
seals peer curiously.

There are no
footpaths from now
on but tractor marks
and sheep trods *Old Roman Catholic Church*
make walking easier. As you go, look for both kinds of
lousewort, sundew, cottongrass, low-growing willow,
butterwort and milkwort. From the shore come the calls of
curlew, black-backed gull, eider and oyster-catcher. Step from
tussock to tussock over the wet parts and then pass through a
gate in the boundary wall.

Bear left to regain the shallow sea cliffs and continue around Camas Stianabhaig. Follow the headland and, as you breast a slope, the huge cliffs of Rùm come into view and then Sanday's sturdy automatic lighthouse.

Stroll on through a purple sward of thyme. Common terns, gulls, geese and shag nest here. The risk of disturbance and predation will be lessened if you stay a hundred yards from the shore and do not linger in this area between late April and the end of July when the birds are most at risk.

From now on the coastline is deeply indented and boulder-strewn. Ahead stand two large stacks, Dùn Beag and Dùn Mór. On these breed fulmar, puffin, kittiwake and guillemot. The calls of the birds fill the air - and the stench of their droppings. Look with care at the caves far below.

Saunter along this lovely high-level southern coastline over thrift, orchis, kidney vetch and the pretty spring squill. At a fence follow the way to cross a gully and then climb the next mound. Here is the site of an Iron-Age fort and you can just discern a circle of stones around a depression.

Leave the fort by the way you climbed up and go on. Look for diminutive rose plants growing on the sloping banks above the bay of Suileabhaig, with white waxy petals almost as large as the individual plant. Stroll on past a wet area on your right, where struggling alders, willows and conifers have been fenced.

Pass through the gate in the wall, taken earlier, and turn left to go on along the high cliffs. On several small islets just offshore, you can see the columnar basalt of which they are composed. Go through the gap in the next wall and stride on. Step across a deepish ditch using a stone causeway and then keep to the higher ground to the right. When a wooden house comes into view, walk right to a gate. Beyond, drop down, left, towards the shore, passing through another gate. Join the track taken earlier on the walk and follow this until you reach the footbridge.

3. A Circular Walk to a Celtic Cross and a Standing Stone on Canna

<table>
<tr><td colspan="2">Information</td></tr>
<tr><td>Distance:</td><td>2 miles from the pier</td></tr>
<tr><td>Time:</td><td>1 hour</td></tr>
<tr><td>Map:</td><td>Pathfinder Canna NG20, Landranger 39 Rùm and Eigg</td></tr>
<tr><td>Terrain:</td><td>Easy walking but strong shoes essential.</td></tr>
</table>

On some days the ferry remains at the pier for an hour. This is a short walk that could be completed in that time.

Follow the track from the pier westwards around the bay. Pass the small building with a cross on its door, now used as the Roman Catholic church, replacing St Edward's mentioned in Walk 2.

Beyond, turn right to walk a cart-track. When the track swings away below an outcrop on the right, walk ahead beside a small planting of deciduous trees full of bird song. Swallows dart overhead and a pair of twite sit on a fence and twitter merrily. Continue to a stile, beyond which stands a ninth-century Celtic cross with one arm missing. Walk on over the site of a ruined village, erased in the

Celtic cross

18

evictions of 1850, to view a standing stone with a small hole in it. Some say it was a punishment stone, others that it might have been used as a calendar.

Go on towards extensive woodland from where a cuckoo calls and then flies over the hill slope. Pass through a gate in the wall and listen for a pair of stonechats scolding on bracken fronds.

Bear right and follow the wall to your right, with a splendid view of Sanday before you. Join a good track into more pleasing woodland, where willow-warblers, chiff chaffs and a black-cap call.

Where the track swings left in front of a house called Tighard, continue ahead with the wall to your right and a fuchsia hedge to the left, to pass through a white metal gate on the right. Go on below an arch of trees, where wild garlic flowers.

Follow the path as it makes a tight zig-zag, and then continue along the outside east wall of Canna House, the home of Dr J L Campbell and his wife, who gave the island to the National Trust for Scotland.

Cuckoo

At the road, turn left. As you return to the pier, leave yourself time to visit the Presbyterian church. Inside the simple undressed stone gives the building a wonderful air of quiet tranquillity. In the graveyard a cross stands above the grave of Alan Gilmour Tom, and his wife, who once owned the island.

4. A Linear Walk to Harris on Rùm

Information	
Distance:	13 long miles
Time:	6 hours
Map:	Pathfinder Rùm (North) NG 30/40, Landranger 39 Rùm and Eigg
Terrain:	Rùm is a rugged island with rough terrain and often adverse weather. Appropriate clothing and equipment is essential.
Access:	Consult access boards at reserve office for details of any temporary restrictions due to conservation management requirements.
Reservations:	Hotel and Hostel, telephone 01687 426037; General enquiries, camping and bothies, telephone 01687 462026.

This is a long hard walk, but the views are spectacular.

Stone crusher

From the front of Kinloch Castle, set off northwards and turn left before the bridge over the Kinloch River. Continue through alder woodland to your right and conifers to your left, from where you can hear the calls of wood and willow warblers and coal, blue and great tits. To your left you can see the peak of

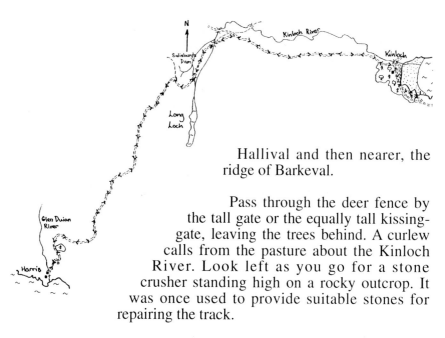

Hallival and then nearer, the ridge of Barkeval.

Pass through the deer fence by the tall gate or the equally tall kissing-gate, leaving the trees behind. A curlew calls from the pasture about the Kinloch River. Look left as you go for a stone crusher standing high on a rocky outcrop. It was once used to provide suitable stones for repairing the track.

At the division of the track, take the left fork and begin the steady climb. Away to your left you can see Long Loch, where red-throated divers swim, and several other smaller sheets of water.

As you continue look for the remains of a dam and a canal, constructed in a vain attempt to channel water towards Kinloch. Lord Salisbury, a sporting landlord of the island during the mid-19th century, wanted to divert the water to improve the salmon fishing. The dam was finished in 1849 but held only for two days and then the water flowed along its old route.

Stride on. Enjoy the view of the Rùm Cuillin with their layered slopes of gabbro. As you begin the long descent towards the ruined village of Harris on the west coast, look for Highland cattle, black and white feral goats and many red deer.

The village of about 30 houses was cleared in 1826 and its people, together with the entire population of the island, were shipped to North America. The residents of Rùm were replaced by 8,000 black-face sheep. Look for the remains of houses and vast areas of lazy-beds about the Glen Duian River. Lazy-beds, for growing potatoes and oats, were formed when shallow soil, often lying over rock, was scraped up into ridges. Seaweed and soot-impregnated thatch was added.

The track ends at Harris Lodge, a shooting lodge where the gillies lived at the back and the sportsmen at the front. The lodge was built by John Bullough, a wealthy industrialist from Lancashire. His son, George Bullough, inherited in 1891 and, ten years later, built Kinloch Castle.

Red deer

Look into the hillside behind the lodge to see the tile-fronted cave where John Bullough was first interred. Later, he was re-interred in a mausoleum in the style of the Parthenon on the edge of wild cliffs near Harris Lodge.

In 1957 Lady Bullough, Sir George's widow, sold Rùm to the nation. It is now in the care of Scottish Natural Heritage and the island has become a national nature reserve. Lady Bullough died in 1969 and was interred beside her husband and father-in-law.

Return by the same route.

5. A Circular Walk towards Guirdil, Rùm

Information

Distance:	12 miles
Time:	8 hours
Map:	Pathfinder Rùm (North) NG 30/40, Landranger 39 Rùm and Eigg
Terrain:	Paths can be rough and wet. The pathless area needs care when crossing the tussocky grass. Do not forget to file your route card at the reserve office.

Leave Kinloch Castle as for Walk 4 and continue to where the track divides. Take the right fork and press along the rough way. Look right towards Kilmory Bay for a dramatic view of Skye.

Canna from Rùm

Cross two burns by small bridges. Beyond, the Kilmory study area is used for research into deer, and access to this

area is normally restricted. Walk the narrow way which climbs left. The springy turf is a great relief after the stony track. Follow the path to continue above a small fenced area of woodland, from where a cuckoo calls.

The path climbs steadily into the heart of the hills. Once over the highest part, begin a gradual descent into Glen Shellesder. Step across several small streams where red damsel flies mate. Here grow two species of sundew, the long-leaved and the round-leaved. Follow the path as it swings south-west. From here there is a wonderful view of the isle of Canna.

Cross the Shellesder Burn by convenient stones above a little waterfall, or wade if necessary, and walk on. Enjoy the grand view down the riven coastline. Press on, now climbing steadily above many lazy-beds. Step or wade across the next burn and go on uphill beside an old turf and stone dyke to your right. Follow this decrepit wall, keeping above and parallel with the Guirdil River. Look across to see an enclosed area of woodland, where another cuckoo calls.

Stroll on beside the wall. Feral goats bleat and feed on the slopes above. Follow the narrow path beside the wall into Glen Guirdil, to pass the foundations of two enclosures on your right. The glen is overshadowed by the towering steep-sided Bloodstone Hill, where ancient man found stone hard enough for crude tools and weapons.

Where the wall ends, begin to bear slightly left over the wet and tussocky turf until you reach the side of a tributary of the burn. Here, in the shelter of the ravine, grow many rowans, laden with large creamy white blossoms, and several aspen trees with leaves quivering in the imperceptible breeze. About the many delightful waterfalls roseroot flowers. This lovely corner of verdant vegetation is just the place to pause on the hard climb through the glen.

Proceed ever upwards, stepping across narrow streams, with meadow pipits, skylarks, several snipes and a pair of kestrels for company, to join the Guirdil path. Here, you could turn right and follow the well-reinforced path up onto Bloodstone Hill, with, on a clear day, a wonderful view awaiting.

To return to Kinloch, turn left on the path and go on climbing to the Bealach a' Bhràigh Bhig, from where there is a tremendous view *Round-leaved* back to Sanday and *sundew* ahead to the Red and Black Cuillin of Skye.

Long-leaved sundew

Follow the good path over the pass, where a herd of Highland cattle feeds. Then drop down across the flatter area about the stream, Abhainn Monadh Mhiltich. The reinforced path is still wet in parts. At Malcolm's Bridge, turn left and follow the track back to Kinloch, passing the remains of Lord Salisbury's dam (see Walk 4).

6. A Circular Walk through Kinloch Glen, Rùm

Information	
Distance:	2 ½ miles
Time:	1 ½ hours
Map:	Pathfinder Rùm (North)NG 30/40,
	Landranger 39 Rùm and Eigg
Terrain:	Generally easy, but some wet areas.

A guide to the Kinloch Glen Nature Trail can be obtained from the reserve office.

Leave Kinloch Castle and cross the meadow, once a lawn belonging to the great house, to the gazebo - the old gate house look-out. Turn left and walk along the path by the shore. Pass the post office, the oldest inhabited building on Rùm, and once the kitchen of Kinloch House. Originally occupied by the laird of the island, Kinloch House was demolished after the castle was built. Go on past a small house in a clump of trees, the former dairy.

Northern eggar moth

Cross the bridge over the Kinloch River and turn left through a gate to stroll a track shaded by willow, ash, oak, rhododendron and lodge-pole pine. Beyond the wooded area, turn right and follow a track up through pasture, where ragged robin and marsh orchid

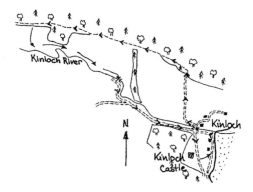

grow. Willow and wood warblers call and curlews fly
overhead uttering their plaintive cries.

Pass through a gate in the wall and bear left to walk through
more alder, willow, oak, hazel and wild cherry. Enjoy the
magnificent view of the path to Dibidil (Walk 9) and to Coire
Dubh (Walk 8). A golden-ringed dragonfly flits over the
herbage.

Go on by a plantation on the left, which stretches down to
the river. As you pass a small burn, large bushes of broom
perfume the air. Look for northern eggar moth caterpillars
crawling over the grass. Snipe fly up from the muddy areas.

Just beyond the straggly woodland on the left, look for a
rusty gate in the wall. You now have to return to the river and
find your way to the deer gate. As this book was published,
this part of the route was being developed by Scottish Natural
Heritage, with waymarked stiles and new fences.

The following paragraphs describe the route before these
changes were made. Pass through a gate in the wall and walk
across the pasture to a fence. Turn left and walk with the
lovely river to your right. Step with care over the wet areas
and head on towards duckboarding. Beyond, a stony way
continues. Cross two small streams, where grasshoppers
stridulate. Pass through the next gate and over more
duckboards and walk on over another pasture, still with the
Kinloch River below to the right.

Follow the fence around to a deer gate and, beyond, continue beside the hurrying burn. Sit on a seat, which carries a notice saying it was dedicated to a man who loved to watch birds. Stroll on over more duckboards to cross the river by a footbridge. Proceed along a wide track beside the river where it descends in pretty falls.

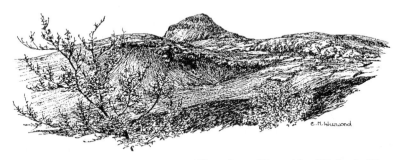

View from Riverside, Kinloch Glen

Emerge onto another track where you turn left to return to the castle.

7. A Linear Walk along South Side, Loch Scresort, Rùm

Information

Distance: 3½ miles
Time: 2 hours
Map: Pathfinder Rùm (North) NG 30/40, Landranger 39
            Rùm and Eigg
Terrain: Path rough in parts. Walking boots advisable.

A guide to South Side Nature Trail can be obtained from the reserve office.

From Kinloch Castle, turn right (south) and walk through trees to the White House, which houses the Nature Reserve office. Join the track that skirts the bay, and pass a limekiln (built in 1850), which supports a good crop of maidenhair spleenwort. The woodland in this area was planted just before the castle was built in 1902. Continue on towards the stone-built pier, which dates from the mid-19th century. It stands on the edge of Loch Scresort, the only deepish-water bay on the island. The Caledonian MacBrayne ferry anchors in the bay and visitors to the island are transferred to the island boat, *Rhouma*, to be

Limekiln

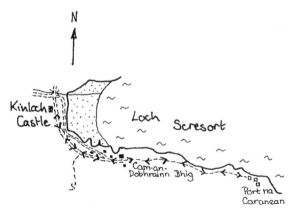

brought to the pier or slipway.

Continue along the road towards the end of the village where a large building doubles as the school and the church. Turn right and climb the slope. At the top, turn left and walk on to take an arrowed path on the right.

Otter

Stroll through the trees and out onto moorland, where purple moor-grass, deergrass, cottongrass and heather grow, all typical of an acidic soil. Look for the many small rowans and birches emerging from the low-growing vegetation. Sheep were removed from the island in 1957 to reduce grazing pressure and deer are kept back behind deer fences. As a result these young trees thrive.

Press on into shady woodland and watch left for a solitary grave. Here is buried a seaman from a cargo ship, who drowned in 1928. On the grave moss, wood sorrel and ferns flourish. Several ruined cottages stand among trees where red-breasted mergansers nest.

Follow the path down onto a pebble beach overlooking Loch Scresort; here, boats lie at anchor and female eiders tend their young. Look across to the Skye Cuillin with the low-lying island of Soay in front.

As you move into more woodland, look for several aspen trees and listen to their trembling leaves. Descend a rougher part of the track onto the pebbled shore of Carn-an-dobhrain Bhig, meaning cairn of the little otter. At the right time of the day you may indeed see an otter.

Go on along the path over moorland to the ruined village of Port-na-Caranean. Five families of crofters moved here from Skye in 1827 after the people of Rùm were shipped to Nova Scotia in 1826. Now among the ruins nest common and lesser black-backed gulls. Oyster-catchers, sandpipers and herring gulls nest on the shore. Between April and July you are asked to proceed no further because of the nesting birds.

Return the same way.

8. A Linear Walk to Coire Dubh, Rùm

Information

Distance:	3 miles
Time:	1 ½ hours
Map:	Pathfinder Rùm (North) NG 30/40, Landranger 39
	Rùm and Eigg
Terrain:	A steady climb over a clear but stony way.

Leave Kinloch Castle and walk right, south. Take the stile, signposted Coire Dubh, on the right, just before the sandstone bridge over the Allt Slugan a' Choilich. The stile gives access to a lawn spangled with buttercups, daisies and orchis at the side of the castle. To the left flows the dancing burn. Continue through the lovely woodland to pass through a gate. Go on, keeping left of the generator house. In the trees close by a family of long-tailed tits chatters and scolds.

Pass out of the trees onto the open hillside and climb the good path through great banks of heather and hard fern. The way continues ever upwards beside the hurrying water. Here, in the shelter of the gill, thrive rowan, willow and Scots pine.

Sea eagle mobbed by ravens

After a steady ascent, you come to the first dam built on the river by Sir George Bullough, owner of the castle, to

33

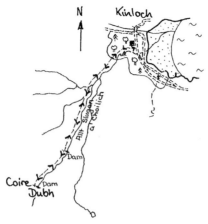

improve his water supply. Bear right to pass through a gate in the deer fence, then return, left, to the side of the river. The path continues to climb until a second dam, now breached, is reached. The low wall of stones is set on the edge of a wide grassy coire, overlooked by the lower slopes of Barkeval and Hallival.

Sit in this quiet hollow in the hills and watch for a sea eagle. This large pale-headed and white-tailed bird soars overhead quite unconcerned by the mobbing of five ravens. When they do fly off, it soars away over the mountain tops.

The Cuillin of Skye from Coire Dubh

Return by the same route and, as you go, enjoy the grand views over Kinloch, the northern end of Rùm and northwards to Skye.

9. A Linear Walk to Dibidil, Rùm

Information	
Distance:	11 or 15 miles
Time:	6 or 8 hours
Map:	Pathfinder Rùm (North) NG 30/40, Rùm (South) NM 261 38/48, Landranger 39 Rùm and Eigg
Terrain:	This is a long hard walk with spectacular views.

Leave Kinloch Castle and walk right (south) to pass the reserve office. Go along the track through pleasing woodland, where coal tits and goldcrests call from conifers and rhododendrons. Stride through the magnificent white gates and walk on to take the signposted right turn for Dibidil. Continue on the stony path.

The path leads steadily upwards through heather moorland. Look for the great flat outcrops of rock used as anvils by hoodie crows and gulls for smashing and eating crustaceans.

Watch for the small signpost directing you right at the division of paths. As you climb, you might see a cuckoo flying low over the moor. Here grows purple moor grass, cottongrass, heather, deergrass, and rushes interspersed with cushions of sphagnum moss. Bog asphodel is in bud. Both common and pale butterwort thrive and all three species of sundew flourish.

The path comes close to a small stream, where rowan,

willow and honeysuckle
grow. Scattered sparsely
over the slopes are small
birches, shrub willow and alder.
Then you come to the deer gate and
realise that from now on you will see
few trees.

Look for the delightful waterfalls
on the Allt Mór na h-Uamha and
then step, or wade, across the
hurrying water. Go on along the
path and suddenly the isle of
Eigg comes into view across the
Sound of Rùm. First you see the
craggy sides of Beinn Bhuidhe and
then the huge distinctive top of An
Sgurr. Beyond lie the mainland
mountains.

Stroll the clear path to cross Allt na
h-Uamha, again using convenient
boulders, or wading. Look upstream
for more foaming waterfalls. As
you follow the path around the
lower slopes of Beinn nan
Stac, the low-lying isle
of Muck comes into
view, with Beinn Airein
standing tall and square.
Further on you pass, on
the left, Lochan Dubh.

Enjoy the grand views and then follow the path downhill to
cross Allt-nam-Bà. Look for a plummeting waterfall where
the silvery burn hurtles over boulders and then the side of a
ravine in its ecstatic leap to reach the sea.

Follow the path as it climbs steadily, winding round the
skirts of the mountain. Then the path comes close to the edge
of high cliffs and care is required. Look for the green top of a

stack, lower than the path, where black-backed gulls nest. The path then moves inland, passing through bracken and steadily descending to the Dibidil River, which you ford. Continue ahead to the Dibidil bothy at the mouth of Glen Dibidil.

From outside the bothy, on the grassy sward, you have a dramatic view of the slopes of Askival, Trollaval, Hallival and Ainshval cradling the glen. The bothy is a restored crofthouse for use by anyone wishing to stay overnight in the interior of the island. Close by are the ruins of other crofthouses and collecting pens - an idyllic corner in the summer sun.

Waterfall - Allt-nam-Bà

Manx shearwaters

Walk down towards the bay, where the Dibidil River descends in a fine waterfall. A pair of sandpipers nests nearby and the male calls from a neighbouring boulder. Out on the waters of the sound, hundreds of Manx shearwaters float and chatter. After dark they return to their burrows and their solitary young, high on the mountain tops.

Walkers with plenty of time can continue to Papadil, a further two miles along the track.

Return by the same route. From the path you have a spectacular view of the Cuillin of Skye and of the mainland, with the houses of Mallaig showing white and clear.

10. A Linear Walk to Kildonnan, Eigg

Information

Distance: 3 miles
Time: 1-2 hours
Map: Pathfinder 261 NM 38/48 Eigg, Muck and Rùm
(South), Landranger 39 Rùm and Eigg
Terrain: Generally easy, but strong footwear required.

Leave the pier by the only road and follow it as it skirts Galmisdale Bay. To the left stands deciduous woodland and in the ditch below the road water avens grows, shading from gold to deep pink. Just beyond Shore Cottage, take the track leading right. Look right to see the disused Clanranald Pier, left high and dry when the tide ebbs and often underwater at high tide. Above, on a knoll, a family of hooded crows chatters.

Clanranald harbour

39

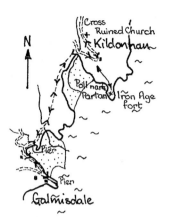

Stroll on along the track, which is shaded by hazel, oak, wych elm and ash. Step across the Allt Eas Chuthain and then stride on over pasture, where lousewort, pink orchis, flags and silverweed flower. Continue ahead to a gap in the wall. (Ignore the gate in the fence on the left.)

Keep to the path that runs parallel with the bracken to your right. Where the path divides, take the right branch up the slope. Step across the next little stream and walk on, with the bracken and fenced cliff edge to your right. Climb to the fence post at the highest point and then go ahead for a hundred yards, with care, and through a convenient gap on your right. Remnants of a stile lie on the ground.

Beyond, walk circumspectly close to the cliff edge, steadily descending into hazel woodland, where foxgloves, vetch, pink campion and primroses flower. Pass through a small gate and saunter on through flags and bluebells. Eiders and sandpipers call from the bay, Poll nam Partan, below. Follow the path as it continues below a cliff of magnificent basalt columns to the road.

Turn right, passing an old cornmill, with the remains of its huge waterwheel. Stride on, keeping to the right of Kildonnan Farmhouse, and walk out to the site of an Iron-Age fort, where stones still border a depression. A smaller stone circle lies beside it. The Picts are said to have constructed this defensive dun.

St Donnan, who introduced Christianity to Eigg, is thought to have occupied the fort while monks built a wooden church on the hill, on the site of the present graveyard.

Leave the fort and return past the farm. Take the upper of

two tracks to visit the ruined church and graveyard. There is a schist cross (probably 15th-century) by the graves. It has lost its cross head, which was a replacement, and this lies at the foot of the shaft. The new graveyard lies close by. Beyond lies the picturesque roofless church, yellowed with lichen and overgrown with weeds.

Eiders

To return you may like to cross the sands, if the tide is out. If not, return by the same route.

11. A Circular Walk from the Pier to An Sgurr and Cleadale, Eigg

Information

Distance:	11 miles
Time:	5-6 hours
Map:	Pathfinder 261 NM 38/48 Eigg, Muck and Rùm (South), Landranger 39 Rùm and Eigg
Terrain:	Good paths, except for the virtually pathless way through Gleann Charadail. Here, after rain, the heather can be wet and the sphagnum hold much water. Leggings or overtrousers and strong boots advisable.

If time is short because of ferries, the walk from the pier to An Sgurr and back will take between three and four hours. Or you could take a taxi (ask at the shop at the pier) to Galmisdale House and walk from there to the top and back (2½ hours).

Walk the only road from the pier for 100 yards and, when the way divides, take the left fork, a metalled track. Follow it uphill through the glorious woodland about the Lodge. Pass through a gate over the track and continue through a flower-strewn field. The path takes you past the sturdy but dilapidated Galmisdale House on your left.

Turn left to join an unmade road coming in on your right. After 50 yards, take the grassy trod that climbs, right, between bracken and heather. Go on climbing the good path and enjoy

the magnificent views. Look up at the awesome pitchstone ridge of An Sgurr and then follow the path as it curves round to the north of the majestic basalt lump.

Look for orchis, milkwort, tormentil and mountain everlasting as you climb steadily. Grouse droppings are the only evidence of the birds. Try your echo as you walk.

The path leads south to a gully between high walls of basalt. At the head of a narrow defile is a cairn. Just beyond, begin your scramble up the rocky slope to your left. Follow the clear path after your scrambling with a grand view of the island of Muck, far below. Pause as you go to see immediately below you, but far down, the only visible building on the wide grassy plateau. Once Grulin had two settlements, and it is possible to trace the foundations of many houses. In the far distance you can see the islands of Coll, Tiree and Mull and the shoreline of Ardnamurchan.

Walk on over the basalt pavement, keeping to the left of a small lochan. Look for a pair of kestrels, which nest on the nearby rocks. Walk with care over the cobbled top of An Sgurr and then scramble, left, to the triangulation point (1,289 feet). Here, a great view awaits of the Cuillin of Rùm and of Skye, and the Torridons.

As you return by the same route, look ahead and down to lonely Loch nam Ban Móra, with its small island. Descend by the cairn, through the gully of rock, and ahead across the sheep trod through the heather to the loch. Edge along the right (north) shore of this delightful expanse of water, or through the heather above. The island, possibly a crannog, was believed to have been constructed and fortified by the Picts. They were small people and many could crowd on the island in times of trouble, keeping themselves warm with peat fires. Today the loch is inhabited by a pair of red-throated divers.

Bear right at the end of the loch to join a path that comes close to Loch Caol na Cora-bheinne. Stroll round the shore to see more of the pretty loch as it stretches away right, below Cora-bheinne, which is a wonderful exposure of columnar basalt.

Red-throated divers

Begin to descend, keeping close to the narrow burn, Abhainn Gleann Chàradail. Walk the narrow strip of green pasture about the fine stream. Great areas of heather, with an understorey of sphagnum, stretch away to hills on either side. Move from one side to another of the narrow rivulet to find the easiest way to tackle this challenging part of the walk. Make full use of sheep trods.

In early summer, look out for cuckoos flying up the gill - head-height. Continue down Gleann Chàradail. Keep well above an attractive fall, as the sheep do. Then the heather becomes shorter and a narrow path leads left along a low ridge. Stay on this and follow the contours round above an extensive area of willow woodland. While remaining on high-level ground, cross the burn at the point just before the stream begins to descend a steep-sided gorge.

Beyond, stride a much clearer path to pass through a large circle of short bracken, with circles of stones nearby, possibly ruined huts. The path passes through a grassy gully and as you climb out of this you can see Cleadale and the extensive afforestation in the centre of the island. And then the glorious Bay of Laig, with its blue, blue water rolling over golden sand, comes into view.

Go on until you reach a fence. Follow it left to join a path zig-zagging steeply down to Laig (once a largish settlement). Join the track that passes right of the farmhouse. Look here for grey wagtails, sandpipers and house martins flying low over a small stream, the same one that you followed down through the glen.

An Sgurr

Continue along the track to a stile to the glorious sands where cattle paddle and, further along, families swim.

Leave the bay by a track that leads to a Roman Catholic church, which you might like to visit. Then walk on along the shallow cliffs of sculptured sandstone, with dykes of dolerite striking seaward. Enjoy a dramatic view of the island of Rùm.

As you near Camas Sgiotaig, 'Singing Sands Bay', keep inside the fence along the higher cliffs. Follow the path inside the fence, the only safe way down to the shore. Walk left round and below a tremendous overhanging cliff. Immediately left of it is a natural arch and a canyon, a great place for children to explore.

Left (south) of this area, scuff the sands when dry to make them sing. It is more of a squeak than a song: the pressure of your boots forces out air trapped between the quartz grains. Here a solitary ringed plover pipes plaintively.

Return to the top of the cliffs by the same path and then strike diagonally left over rough pasture in the direction of the pinnacle ('God's Finger') on Beinn Bhuidhe. At the fence, follow it right to join a wide fenced way to the left of a bungalow.

Join the road and walk on. Just past the junction of roads is Cleadale Crafts, a renovated crofthouse, where you can get a refreshing cup of tea. Climb the hill to Bealach Clithe, where a path, a short cut from Laig, joins the road.

Enjoy this quiet narrow road as it continues through the island, passing the shop and post office on its way. Beyond the school, keep to the right branch of the road, to continue to the pier.

12. A Circular Walk to Two Caves on Eigg

Information

Distance:	2 miles
Time:	2 hours
Map:	Pathfinder 261 NM 38/48 Eigg, Muck and Rùm (South), Landranger 39 Rùm and Eigg
Terrain:	Easy walking, but strong shoes or boots essential on the way down to the caves.

Leave the pier and, where the road divides, take the metalled track as far as for Walk 11. Go through the woodland about The Lodge and pass the entrance to the estate on your right. Stroll on to take a metal gate on the left to walk a track. Look on the right of the way for an old well. Keep to the left of the house and take the left of the two tracks, leading away from the house.

Cathedral Cave

Press on, keeping parallel with the cliff edge but about 100 yards inland. Cross a stile and descend the next gully. A narrow path continues along the grassy skirt of the great cliffs. It drops steadily to the shore and then after a little scrambling you reach the entrance to Cathedral Cave. This huge lofty cavern, where drips descend in a curtain, was used for illicit services after the Reformation, when Roman Catholicism was banned. If the tide is right, you can sit and watch an otter at play, but the entrance to the cave can be under water at times.

Return along the narrow path to the gully and then descend to the shore and turn left. Walk on for a few yards and look up above a gently-sloping greensward to see a low narrow opening. This is the entrance to Massacre Cave where more than 300 MacDonalds perished. All but one of the people of Eigg were hiding there from the MacLeods of Skye who were bent on retribution after a particularly nasty deed by the MacDonalds. Once the cave had been discovered, the MacLeods built a huge bonfire and suffocated everyone. After an initially low 20-foot entrance, the cave opens out into a large cavern.

Climb back up the gully and return along the edge of the cliffs, walking through a magnificent flower garden. Press on through bracken and then follow the path as

Yellow flags

it swings inland for a few yards. Use a plank bridge to cross a small stream that flows through the gill, lush with oak, willow and flags.

A few yards on, watch for the place that the track drops right, through bracken, and then continues in the same general direction, below willow scrub, to a stile. Walk on a few yards and then swing right to descend a rough stony way that drops towards the sea. it is easy to miss this turn when the bracken is high. It lies just beyond mixed woodland that hugs a huge bluff of rock. From here the way, often wet, continues over meadows to the pier.

13. A Circular Walk from the Pier to climb Beinn Airein, Muck

Information	
Distance:	4 ½ -5 miles
Time:	2-3 hours
Map:	Pathfinder 261 NM 38/48 Eigg, Muck and Rùm (South), Landranger 39 Rùm and Eigg
Terrain:	Generally easy but the going can be wet in places. Steep climb to Beinn Airein. Take care on very high cliffs.

Stride the road from the pier to pass a stone house and then the excellent craft shop and tea room. Continue to the graveyard and climb to the prominent stone-built memorial, commemorating three people drowned near Horse Island. They were shooting shags. Above the graveyard is the ruined village of Keil, which was deserted at the time of the Clearances in 1828.

Climb straight uphill and turn left to Caisteal an Dùin Bhain, a rock, once fortified, on the promontory overlooking Port Mór. Head on round towards inland cliffs, to the left of a small unobtrusive plantation of mixed conifers. Use helpful sheep trods to reach the cairn on Fionn-aird, from where there is a spectacular view.

Herons

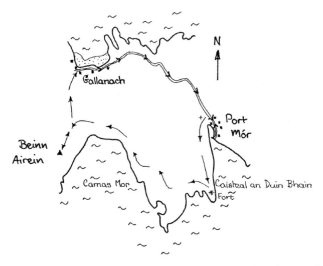

Stroll along the high cliffs that curve round a dramatic bay of black basalt boulders and crags. Cross the fence at a suitable place and go on above the bay of Fang Mór. Pass through the gate. Strike uphill along a track. Away to the right is a wet area where a pair of heron fish.

At the wall, walk right to its north end, to pass through a gate by a pleasing stone sheepfold. Keep by the fence, ignoring the stile over it and follow the fence until you can pass through a gate on your right. This takes you inside the fence, which is now on your left.

Continue uphill, the fence still edging the sheer cliffs to your left. This involves a steepish climb over grass. Where the fence ends at a flaring cliff, take a stony trod up the slope on the right. This brings you to the cairn on Beinn Airein - the highest point on the island (451 feet). On a good day you can see Coll, Tiree, the Treshnish Isles, Iona, Mull, the Mainland, Skye, Eigg, Rùm, Canna, South Uist, Barra, Vatersay and Eriskay. The summit cliffs drop sheer almost to the sea at Camas Mór, the island's Site of Special Scientific Interest. On these cliffs nest many seabirds.

Leave by the route taken to the top and at the fence climb the good stile and head on over the pasture, left, to a gate in

51

the corner. Beyond, turn right to stroll downhill, with the fence to you right. When you reach a very wet hollow, circle left and then right to return to the fence.

Climb the slope and then follow a tractor path. Keep well to the left of a small deciduous copse. The tractor path joins the farm track and swings right to the farm buildings at Gallanach.

Eigg from Muck

Pass through the gate and then turn right to join the metalled road. On your left are some fine sandy beaches. Walk the road through the lovely island. It is traffic-free and cattle graze contentedly in pastures. There are hay meadows to your left. Press on to the pier.

14. A Linear Walk to see Horse Island, Muck

Information	
Distance:	3½ miles
Time:	1½ -2 hours (this does not include visiting Horse Island)
Map:	Pathfinder 261 NM 38/48 Eigg, Muck and Rùm (South), Landranger 39 Rùm and Eigg
Terrain:	Easy walking but there are several wet areas to be crossed with care.

Leave the pier by the only road. Pass the craft shop and tea room. Beyond is a white building that houses the island's diesel generators. Continue past, on your left, the graveyard and the stone memorial close to the village of Keil, abandoned during the Clearances. Follow the road for just over a mile to pass the farmhouse at Gallanach, which has pleasing sandy beaches opposite.

Old crofthouse

53

Saunter along the continuing narrow path below the ribbed basalt cliffs, where foxglove, ivy, veronica and wild rose grow. Take the stile on the left, just before a cottage and climb straight up the low cliffs. Go ahead, following an indistinct narrow path that has helpful planks and stones to aid you over the wet patches. Aim for the crofthouse, following the contours round an old dyke.

Horse Island

N

Aird nan Uan

Gallanach

Muck

Port Mòr

The tiny listed building has been restored and has a turf roof. In front grow water avens and ragged robin. Meadow pipits and wheatears busy themselves about the stones and turf of the house. Go on above the boggy ground to a small bay with a beach composed entirely of small shells. Return to the listed building and around the next little bay to pass through a gate in the ruined stone wall, the latter with a hog hole in it. Common blue butterflies flit about the flowers.

Take care as you walk not to disturb a snipe nesting by the path. Its four fawn-coloured eggs, with black markings, lie in a deep pocket of grass. Ahead, on the site of a Bronze-Age burial circle, stand stones commemorating MacEwens buried here.

Beyond is the way to Horse Island. Climb onto Lamb Island first and then scramble over seaweed-covered rocks. This can be attempted only at low water at spring tides. (Ask at Gallanach for exact times.)

Return along the low cliffs, overlooking Gallanach Bay. Two horses sculpted in driftwood and set on posts, point towards Horse Island. Seals call mournfully from the shallow water below and overhead fly grey-lag geese.

Don't miss the way down by the cottage; the latter is hidden by the cliff. Walk the path and then the road to return to the pier.

Common blue

15. A Circular Walk round the Eastern End of Muck

Information	
Distance:	2½ miles
Time:	1½ hours
Map:	Pathfinder 261 NM 38/48 Eigg, Muck and Rùm (South), Landranger 39 Rùm and Eigg
Terrain:	Easy walking but strong footwear required.

Leave the pier as for Walk 14. Walk to the sharp bend, just under a mile from the start, at the point where the road comes close to the sandy shore of Camas na Cairidh. Leave the road, right, to pass through a gateless gap in the wall. Stroll to the top right corner to go through a second gate. Continue left over the ridge with the cliff on the left. Here sheep, including a Jacob tup, graze. Cross the second fence where there are no barbs.

Walk left, edging the hay meadow on its seaward side. Overhead common gulls call. Cross the wall by keeping along the shore. Go on over rough pastures, from where you can see Grulin on Eigg. Keep left of the high ground ahead and left of the fence.

Pass through a gate by a sheep pen and walk on by a small lochan, almost overgrown by bog bean. Go round the next bay to pass a ruined building. Cross a deep

Bog bean

ditch, which requires a large step, or keep on the shore if this presents difficulties.

Walk a sheep trod, bearing right and following the contours around a hillock. Pass through a turf and stone dyke and go on along the trod, keeping above a very wet area. Here you can still see the outlines of lazy-beds. This area was once under intensive cultivation. Continue to a gate in the fence, where you are asked to 'Keep it Shut'.

Proceed along the contours, keeping above another wet area, where ragged robin, flags, bog myrtle, reeds and orchids grow. Step across the ditch (easier this time) and follow the trod around the fence.

Harbour

When the radio masts come into view, head towards them, picking the driest way. Join a wide reinforced track to the site of a future wind generator. From here, drop down the slope towards the houses around the pier, keeping left of a small clump of conifers, the school and the community hall. Walk on to join the road to the pier.